PULL AHEAD BOOKS

Continents

ASIA

by Madeline Donaldson

Lerner Books • London • New York • Minneapolis

This book was first published in the United States of America in 2005.
First published in the United Kingdom in 2008 by
Lerner Books,
Dalton House,
60 Windsor Avenue,
London SW19 2RR

Website address: www.lernerbooks.co.uk

This edition was updated and edited for UK publication by Discovery Books Ltd., Unit 3, 37 Watling Street, Leintwardine, Shropshire SY7 0LW

Words in **bold type** are explained in a glossary on page 30.

British Library Cataloguing in Publication Data

Donaldson, Madeline
    Asia. - (Pull ahead books. Continents)
    1. Asia - Juvenile literature 2. Asia - Pictorial works
    Juvenile literature
    I. Title
    950

    ISBN-13: 978 1 58013 334 0

Photographs are used with the permission of: ©David Keaton/CORBIS, p. 3; © John Elk III, pp. 6, 15; © Betty Crowell, p. 7; ©Dean Conger/CORBIS, pp. 9, 10–11; © M. Barlow/Art Directors, pp. 12–13; © Art Directors, p. 14; ©Galen Rowell/CORBIS, pp. 16–17; © Victor Englebert, p. 18; © A. A. M. Van der Heyden/Independent Picture Service, p. 19; © A. Tovy/Art Directors, p. 20; © T. Lester/Art Directors, p. 21; © Keren Su/CORBIS, pp. 22–23; © Bachmann/The Image Finders, p. 24; © A. Kuznetsov/Art Directors, p. 25; © Novastock/The Image Finders, pp. 26–27. Maps on pp. 4–5, 8, and 29 by Laura Westlund.

Printed in China

Where can you climb the world's tallest mountain?

The **continent** of Asia! A continent is a big piece of land.

Arctic Ocean

North America

Atlantic Ocean

Pacific Ocean

South America

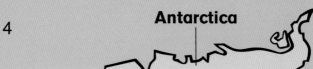

Antarctica

There are seven continents on Earth.
Asia is the largest of all.

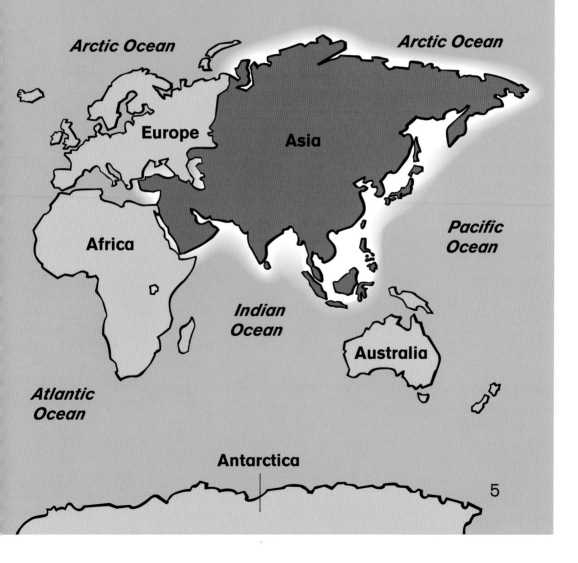

Whoosh! Oceans border Asia on three sides.

Asia's fourth side ends at the low Ural Mountains. These mountains lie between Asia and the continent of Europe.

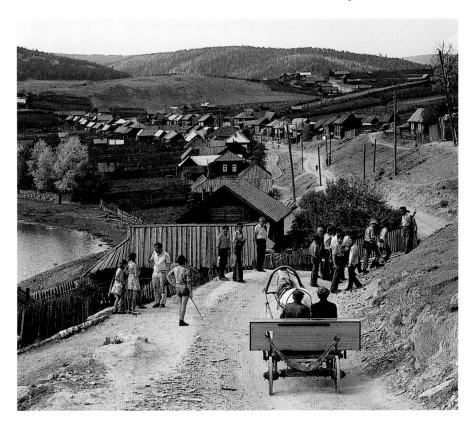

Asia's 49 **countries** are grouped into six **regions.** They are North Asia, Central Asia, South-west Asia, South Asia, South-east Asia and East Asia.

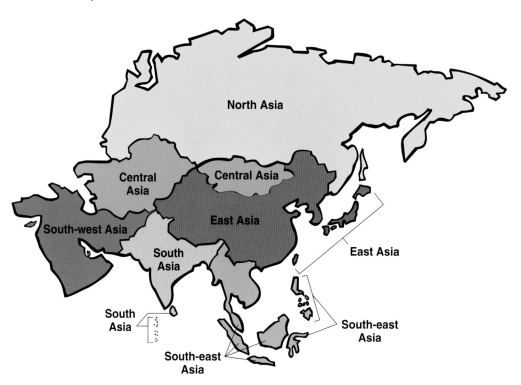

Brrr! Thick snow and ice cover North Asia most of the year. North Asia is also called Siberia.

The cold weather doesn't bother these reindeer in Siberia.

Deserts, mountains and **plateaus,** or high, flat areas, make up Central Asia.

Many of the people of Central Asia
raise animals, such as sheep or goats.

Whew! Deserts also stretch across much of South-west Asia.

The Dead Sea is part of this region. The sea is the lowest place on Earth. People float easily in the sea's salty water.

Many mountain **chains** cut through
South Asia. The Himalaya Mountains
are the tallest.

Do you remember the tallest mountain?
It is called Mount Everest and is part of
the Himalaya chain.

Lots of rain falls on the lands and
islands that make up South-east Asia.

Farmers grow crops of rice in the
region's rich, wet soil.

Large cities are found throughout East Asia. This is Tokyo in Japan.

China is the largest country in East Asia. It has the most people of any country in the world. This is the city of Shanghai in China.

More than three billion people live in all the parts of Asia. They belong to hundreds of **ethnic groups.**

An ethnic group may share the same language and the same religion.

The number of people in South Asia is growing fast. This area may soon have more people than East Asia.

North Asia has the fewest people of any part of Asia. But it has the most land.

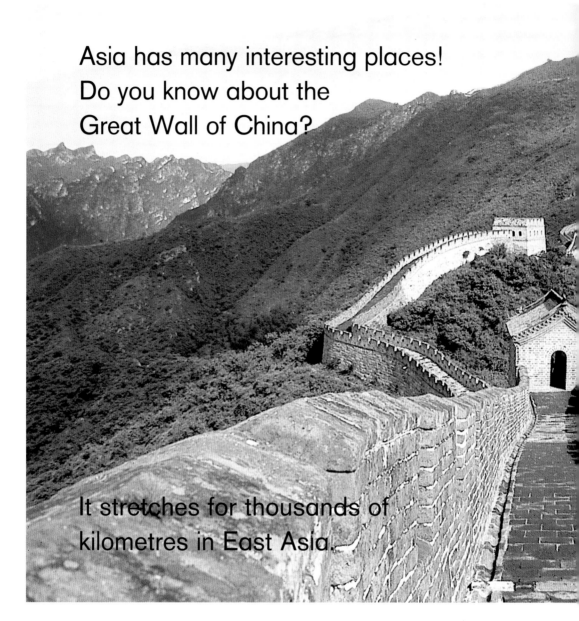

Asia has many interesting places!
Do you know about the
Great Wall of China?

It stretches for thousands of
kilometres in East Asia.

There's always something new to learn about Asia!

Facts about Asia

- Asia covers more than 44 million square kilometres (16 million square miles).

- The large islands of Asia include Borneo, Hainan, Honshu, Luzon, Taiwan and Sakhalin.

- The main rivers of Asia include the River Amur, the River Ganges, the River Huang, the River Mekong, the River Ob and the River Yangtze.

- The animals of Asia include arctic foxes, Asian elephants, camels, giant pandas, tigers and yaks.

- Plants living in Asia include date palm trees, mulberry trees, nutmeg trees and olive trees.

- The large cities of Asia include Bangkok, Beijing, Calcutta, Hanoi, Jerusalem, Manila, Mumbai, Shanghai, Tashkent and Tokyo.

Map of Asia

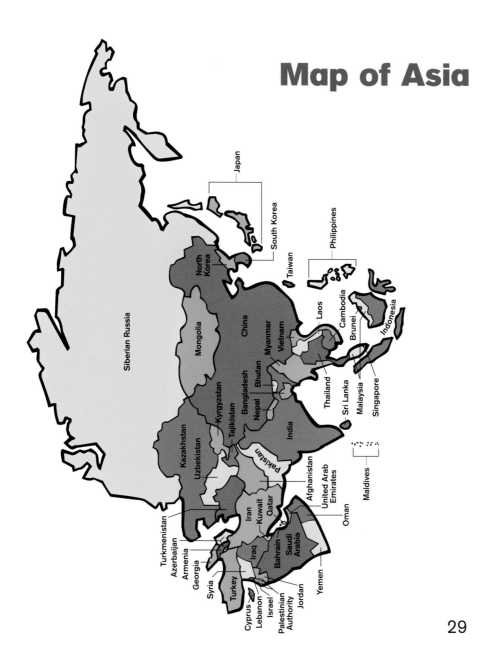

Japan

South Korea

Philippines

Taiwan

North Korea

Siberian Russia

Mongolia

China

Laos

Cambodia

Brunei

Indonesia

Myanmar

Vietnam

Bangladesh

Bhutan

Kyrgyzstan

Tajikistan

Nepal

Thailand

Sri Lanka

Malaysia

Singapore

Kazakhstan

Uzbekistan

Pakistan

India

Afghanistan

United Arab Emirates

Maldives

Turkmenistan

Azerbaijan

Armenia

Georgia

Iran

Kuwait

Qatar

Oman

Syria

Iraq

Bahrain

Saudi Arabia

Yemen

Turkey

Cyprus

Lebanon

Israel

Palestinian Authority

Jordan

29

Glossary

chains: series of linked things. A mountain chain usually makes a long, thick line on a map.

continent: one of seven big pieces of land on Earth

countries: places where people live and share the same laws

ethnic groups: groups of people who have many things in common. They might speak the same language or follow the same religion.

islands: small pieces of land surrounded by water

plateaus: areas of high, flat land

regions: small parts of a larger piece of land

Further Reading and Website

Books

Cumming, David. *Indonesia* (Letters from Around the World) Cherrytree Books, 2004.

Cumming, David. *Pakistan* (Letters from Around the World) Cherrytree Books, 2004.

Das, Prodeepta. *I is for India* Frances Lincoln Children's Books, 2007.

Fisher, Teresa. *A Flavour of Japan* (Food and Festivals) Hodder Wayland, 2002.

Foster, Lelia. *Asia* (Heinemann First Library: Continents) Heinemann Library, 2007.

Ganeri, Anita. *Exploring Asia* (Exploring Continents) Heinemann, 2006.

Powell, Jillian. *China* (Looking at Countries) Franklin Watts, 2006.

Powell, Jillian. *India* (Looking at Countries) Franklin Watts, 2006.

Powell, Jillian. *Japan* (Looking at Countries) Franklin Watts, 2006.

Randall, Ronne. *A Flavour of Israel* (Food and Festivals) Hodder Wayland, 1999.

Senker, Cath. *Saudi Arabia* (Letters from Around the World) Cherrytree Books, 2007.

Enchanted Learning

http://enchantedlearning.com/geography/asia

The geography section of this website has links to every continent.

Index